Milly, Molly
Secret Scarves

"We may look different but we feel the same."

It was the month before Christmas.
"I'm going to knit Molly a scarf," Milly said.
"What a good idea," said Milly's mother.
"Something you make yourself is always special."

"Molly would like a striped one," Milly decided, as her mother sorted through a box of wool and knitting needles.

Milly's mother cast on the stitches and carefully showed Milly how to knit.

Milly sat down with Marmalade and slowly began the first row. She knitted and knitted and knitted. She didn't watch television and she didn't go out to play.
And she didn't tell Molly her secret.

Molly was also thinking about Christmas.
"I'm going to knit Milly a scarf," she said
to her mother.
"Something you make yourself is always special,"
said Molly's mother. "What a good idea."

"Milly likes stripes," said Molly, as her mother
went through her box of wool
and knitting needles.

Molly's mother cast on the stitches and showed her how to knit. Then Molly sat down with Tom Cat and slowly began the first row.

Molly knitted and knitted and knitted.
She didn't watch television and she didn't
go out to play. And she too kept her secret
from Milly.

Milly's scarf grew longer and longer.

And so did Molly's.

On the day before Christmas Milly decided her scarf was long enough. She asked her mother to cast off. "It's not long enough yet," said her mother.

So Milly knitted into the night.

She was still knitting on Christmas morning. "You must love Molly very much," her mother said. "I do," said Milly.

On the day before Christmas, Molly too thought
her scarf was long enough.
She asked her mother to cast off.
"It's not long enough yet," said her mother.

Molly knitted into the night and was still knitting on Christmas morning. "You must love Milly very much," her mother said.
"I do," said Molly.

Finally, Milly's scarf was long enough. She knitted one more row before her mother cast off. "Because," she said, "I love Molly that much more."

Milly wrapped Molly's scarf in red paper
and tied it with a big green bow.

Then she ran out to find Molly.

Finally Molly's scarf was also long enough.
And she too decided to knit one more row.
"Because," she said, "I love Milly that much more."
Her mother cast off.

Molly wrapped Milly's scarf in green paper and tied it with a big red bow.

Then she ran out to find Milly.

Milly and Molly opened their parcels in a flurry of paper and bows and excitement.

"I'm going to wear my scarf always," said Milly. "And I'm going to wear mine forever," said Molly.